YOUR KNOWLEDGE HAS VALUE

AF149187

- - We will publish your bachelor's and master's thesis, essays and papers

- - Your own eBook and book - sold worldwide in all relevant shops

- - Earn money with each sale

Upload your text at www.GRIN.com and publish for free

Massimo Santanicchia

Is globalisation really a global phenomenon?

GRIN Verlag

Bibliografische Information der Deutschen Nationalbibliothek:

Die Deutsche Bibliothek verzeichnet diese Publikation in der Deutschen National-
bibliografie; detaillierte bibliografische Daten sind im Internet über http://dnb.d-
nb.de/ abrufbar.

Imprint:

Copyright © 2002 GRIN Verlag GmbH
Druck und Bindung: Books on Demand GmbH, Norderstedt Germany
ISBN: 978-3-656-42083-5

This book at GRIN:

http://www.grin.com/en/e-book/212644/is-globalisation-really-a-global-phenomenon

GRIN - Your knowledge has value

Der GRIN Verlag publiziert seit 1998 wissenschaftliche Arbeiten von Studenten, Hochschullehrern und anderen Akademikern als eBook und gedrucktes Buch. Die Verlagswebsite www.grin.com ist die ideale Plattform zur Veröffentlichung von Hausarbeiten, Abschlussarbeiten, wissenschaftlichen Aufsätzen, Dissertationen und Fachbüchern.

Visit us on the internet:

http://www.grin.com/

http://www.facebook.com/grincom

http://www.twitter.com/grin_com

Jeorge Fiori | Housing & Urbanism

Is *globalisation* really a global phenomenon?

Massimo Santanicchia | January 2002

Introduction

What does globalization mean? Is it really a global phenomenon? What are the consequences of it in the developed and developing countries?
By studying the book of Saskia Sassen "Cities in a World Economy" and the book of Manuel Castells "The Rise of the Network Society" I try to find answers to my questions.

What is globalization?

Manuel Castells defines the global economy as a new economy.
For him the new economy is informational, global, and networked to identify its fundamental distinctive features and to emphasize their intertwining.
   "It is informational because the productivity and competitiveness of units or agents in this economy fundamentally depend upon their capacity to generate, process, and apply efficiently knowledge-based information. It is global because the core activities of production, consumption, and circulation, as well as their components (capital, labour, raw materials, management, information, technology, markets) are organized on a global scale, either directly or through a network of linkages between economic agents. It is networked because, under the new historical conditions, productivity is generated through and competition is played out in a global network of interaction between business networks."[1]

For Saskia Sassen the notion of a global economy has become deeply entrenched in political and media circles all around the world. Yet its dominant images –the instantaneous transmission of money around the globe, the information economy, the neutralisation of distance through telematics- are partial representations of what really globalization is.
   "What lacks in this abstract model are the material processes, activities, and infrastructures crucial to the implementation of globalization".[2]

One of the most important changes over the last 20 years has been the increase in mobility of capital at both the national and especially the trans-national levels.
This mobility has configured different areas as key-sites in the world economy, while other areas have turned to be obsolete. (Sassen 2000)
   "Increased capital mobility not only brings changes in the geographic organization of manufacturing production and in the network of financial market, but it also generates a demand for types of production needed to ensure the management, control, and servicing of this new organization of manufacturing and finance. The mobility of capital also includes the production of a broad array of innovations in these sectors. These types of production have their own location patterns; they tend toward high levels of agglomeration".[3]

Cities tend to be the places of this concentration.
   "One of the factors influencing the role of cities in the new global economy is the change in the composition of international transactions. The current composition of international transactions shows this transformation very clearly. For instance, foreign direct investment (FDI) grew three times faster in the mid 1980s than the growth of the export trade. Furthermore, by mid 1980s, investment in services had become the main component in FDI flows, whereas before it had been in manufacturing or raw

---

[1] Manuel CAS tells, 1996, The rise of the network society (second edition),
Blackwell Publishers, Oxford,
[2] Saskia Sassed, 2000, Cities in a world economy (second edition),
Pine Forge press, Thousand Oaks, London, Delhi
[3] Saskia Sassen, 2000, Cities in a world economy (second edition),
Pine Forge press, Thousand Oaks, London, Delhi

materials extraction. These trends became even sharper in the 1990s. By 1999, the monetary value of international financial flows was vastly larger than the value of international trade and FDI."[4]

In the 1800s, when the world economy consisted largely of trade of raw materials, agricultural products, or mining goods the crucial sites were harbours, plantations, factories, and mines. Historically, this has meant that a large number of countries in Africa, Latin America, and the Caribbean were key sites in this geography.
Cities were already servicing centres at that time: the major cities typically developed alongside harbours. Trading companies depended on multiple industrial, banking, and other commercial services were also located in cities.
Cities however, were not the key production sites for the leading industries in the 1800s, the production of wealth was centred elsewhere.
When finance and specialized services became the dominant component of international transactions in the early 1980s, the role of cities was strengthened. Today, international trade continues to be an important fact in the global economy, but it has been overshadowed both in value and in power by international financial flows. In the 1980s, finance and specialized services emerged as the major components of international transactions. The crucial sites for these transactions are financial markets, advanced corporate service firms, banks, and the headquarters of trans-national corporations (TNCs). These sites lie at the heart of the process for the creation of wealth, and they are located in cities. (Sassen 2000)

Certainly, harbours continue to be strategic in a world of growing international trade, and also massive industrial districts are in many ways strategic sites for international activity, but they do not really represent what is the world economy today: an economy related more and more to services and financial transactions rather than production and transportation of goods.
According to Saskia Sassen there are three main places that represent the new forms of economic globalization: export processing zones, offshore banking centres, and global cities.

Export processing zones, are areas in low-wage countries where firms from developed countries can locate factories to process and/or assemble components brought in from and re-exported to the developed countries. Special legislation was passed in several developed countries to make this possible. Tax breaks and cheap labour in the zones are additional incentives. These zones are a key mechanism in the internationalisation of production. Powerful company can therefore operate in undeveloped countries avoiding laws and the right of the workers that otherwise they have to respect in their own developed countries.

Offshore financial centres are another important spatial point in the worldwide circuits of financial flows. Such centres are above all else tax shelters, a response by private sector actors to government regulation.
They are located in many parts of the world like in Singapore and Hong Kong, Bahrain, Australia, Mauritius, Switzerland, the Cayman Islands.
Their existence is mainly due to the massive deregulation of major financial markets in the 1980s and the establishment of "free international financial zones".
Compared with the major international centres, offshore banking centres offer certain types of additional flexibility: secrecy, openness to "hot" money and to certain "legitimate" options not quite allowed in the deregulated markets of major financial centres, and tax minimization strategies for international corporations.

---

[4] Saskia Sassen, 2000, Cities in a world economy (second edition),
Pine Forge press, Thousand Oaks, London, Delhi

In brief, offshore banking centres represent a highly specialized location for certain types of international financial transactions. On the broader scale of operations, however, they represent a fraction of the financial capital markets now concentrated in global cities.

"Global cities are strategic sites for the management of the global economy and the production of the most advanced services and financial operations. They are key sites for the advanced services and telecommunications facilities necessary for the implementation and management of global economic operations. They also tend to concentrate the headquarters of firms, especially firms that operate globally.
The growth of international investment and trade and the need to finance and service such activities have fed the growth of these functions in major cities. The erosion of the role of the government in the world economy, which was much larger when trade was the dominant form of international transaction, has displaced some of the organizing and servicing work from governments and major headquarters to specialised service firms and global markets in services and finance.
They also are marketplaces where firms and governments from all over the world can buy financial instruments and specialized services".[5]

---

[5] Saskia Sassen, 2000, Cities in a world economy (second edition),
Pine Forge press, Thousand Oaks, London, Delhi

Does *globalization* exist?

"The world economy has never been a planetary event; it has always had more or less clearly defined boundaries. After the Second World War until the 70s the United States represented the dominant country in the political, cultural and economical scene. With the reconstruction of the economies in Western Europe and Japan we assisted a new phase of the world economy. A limited but growing number of major cities are the sites for the major financial markets and leading specialized service firms, while some other cities have lost their role as leading export centres for manufacturing, precisely because of the decentralization of production."[6]

A global economy according to Castells is an economy with the capacity to work as a unit in real time, or chosen time, on a planetary scale.

"We can assert that there is a global economy because economies around the world depend on the performance of their globalized core. This globalized core includes financial market, international trade, trans-national production, and, to some extent, science and technology, and specialty labour.
It is through these globalized, strategic components of the economy that the economic system is globally interconnected"[7]

If we look up in the dictionary, we find the followings definitions:
Global *adj.* **1.** pertaining to the whole world; world-wide; universal: *the dream of global peace.* **2.** comprehensive **3.** globular, or globe-shaped. **4.** of, pertaining to, or using a terrestrial or celestial globe. (Webster's encyclopedic unabridged dictionary of the English language, 1989, Portland House, New York)
Global *adj* **1.** concerning or including the whole world **2.** involving or relating to all the parts or aspects of a situation. (Collins English Dictionary, 1987, Collins, London)
Global *adj* **1.** Having the shape of a globe, spherical. **2.** Of, relating to, or involving the entire earth; worldwide: *global war; global monetary policies.* **3.** Comprehensive, total: *"a . . . global, generalized sense of loss"* (Maggie Scarf). **4.** *Computer Science* Of or relating to an entire program, document, or file. (The American Heritage® Dictionary of the English Language: Fourth Edition. 2000).

Accordingly to these definitions can we still talk about a *global* economy?

It is true that the new economy is informational, networked is based on the mobility of capital and international financial flows; But is this really enough to define the new economy as global?

We also have to consider that the
"Decisive agents in setting up a new, global economy were governments, and, particularly the governments of the wealthiest countries, the G-7 (the USA, the UK, Japan, Canada, France, Germany and Italy), and their ancillary international institutions, the International Monetary Fund, the World Bank, and the World Trade Organization."[8]
Therefore it cannot be exactly defined as the whole world.

If we look at some data we can then understand that "Along the worldwide expansion of international trade, there has been a trend toward relative diversification of the areas of trade. In 1965 exports between developed economies accounted for 59% of the total, but in 1995, the proportion had been reduced to 47%, while the corresponding figure for exports between developing countries increased from 3.8% to 14.1%. This broadening of the geographical basis of international trade must be qualified, however, by several considerations.
First, developed economies continue to be the overwhelming partners in international trade.

---

[6] Saskia Sassen, 2000, <u>Cities in a world economy (second edition)</u>,
Pine Forge press, Thousand Oaks, London, Delhi
[7] Manuel Castells, 1996, <u>The rise of the network society (second edition)</u>,
Blackwell Publishers, Oxford
[8] Manuel Castells, 1996, <u>The rise of the network society (second edition)</u>,
Blackwell Publishers, Oxford

Second, while the share of developing countries in manufacturing exports has substantially increased, from 6% in 1965 to 20% in 1995, still leaves 80% for developed countries.
Third, developed countries overwhelmingly dominate trade in high-value, high technology products.
Finally the developed countries export 71% of the world's total exports of goods and services, while accounting for only 19% of the world's population".[9]

The new economy from one hand is deeply linked with the entire world but on the other hand it is not managed and controlled by all the countries, precisely just a very limited number of nations (mainly the G-7) hold the key to the global economy, and they decide which countries participate to the planetary economy and on what terms.
If we consider then the foreign direct investments FDI, by the mid-1980s, 75% of all FDI stock and 84% of FDI stock in services was in developed countries.
There was a sharp concentration even among developed countries in these patterns:
The top four recipient countries (United States, United Kingdom, France and Germany) accounted for half of world inflows in the 1980s.
The five major exporters of capital (United States, United Kingdom, Japan, France and Germany) accounted for 70% of total outflows.
Financial concentration is evident in a ranking of the top 30 banks in the world, with only eight countries represented: Japan, Germany, France, Switzerland, The Netherlands, The United Kingdom, the United States and China. (*Source:* Based on *Hoover's Handbook of World Business* 1998)

The amount and the direction of the FDI towards the developing countries has changed remarkably in the last twenty years and today it is difficult to define a trustful trend.
International investment in developing countries lost share in the 1980s, although it increased in absolute value, than regained share by the early 1990s and lost it again in the mid 1990s.
Also the destination of these FDI is volatile, between 1985 and 1989, Latin America's share of total flows to developing countries fell from 49% to 38%, and Southeast Asia's share rose from 37% to 48%.
If we organize some of the evidence on financial flows according to the places where the markets and firms are located, we can see distinct patterns of concentration. The evidence on the location of banks and securities houses points to sharp concentration.
For example, the worldwide distribution of the 100 largest banks and 25 largest securities houses in 1991 shows that Japan, the United States, and the United Kingdom accounted for 39 and 23% each, respectively. (Sassen 2000)

---

[9] Manuel Castells, 1996, The rise of the network society (second edition),
Blackwell Publishers, Oxford

Cities Ranked by Assets of the World's Top 50 Largest Commercial Banks, 1997 (US$ millions)

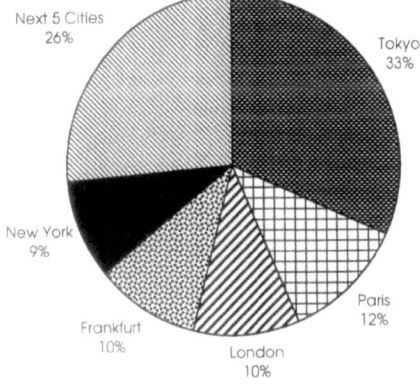

Source: Based on "World Business," *Wall Street Journal*, September 22, 1989; "World Business," *Wall Street Journal*, September 28, 1998.

If we consider then the share of world stock market the 75% of it is divided among the United States, the United Kingdom and Japan while the 25% represent the share of the rest of the world. (*Source:* Based on Meridian Securities Markets, *World Stock Exchange Fact Book* 1998)

Top Cities Ranked by Stock Market Value, 1990 and 1997 (US$ billions)

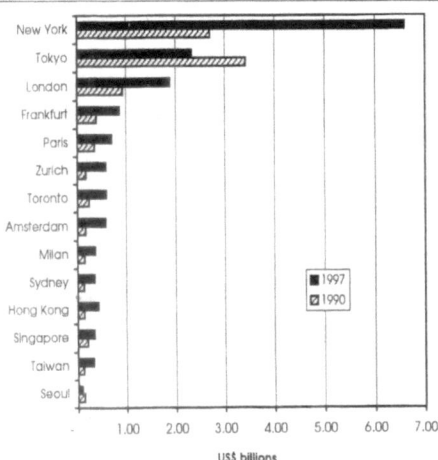

Source: Based on Meridian Securities Markets, *World Stock Exchange Fact Book* (1998).
Note: For Australia 1997, the number of listed companies is from 1996; when only domestic is listed, it represents the total market value.

Also the stock market transaction is concentrated in few cities:
Tokyo's exchange market accounts for 90% of equities trading in Japan. New York accounts
for about two-thirds of equities trading in the United States; and London accounts for most
trading in the United Kingdom. (Sassen 2000)

U.S. Cities Ranked by Assets of 100 Largest Commercial
Banking Companies, 1992 (US$ millions)

City	Assets	Percentage of U.S. Top 100
Total, Top 100 U.S. Firms	2,500,315	—
New York	715,065	28.6
San Francisco	263,508	10.5
Chicago	109,761	4.4
Los Angeles	58,163	2.3
Total of above cities	1,146,497	45.9

Rank	City	Assets
1	New York	715,065
2	San Francisco	263,508
3	Charlotte, NC	169,386
4	Chicago	109,761
5	Pittsburgh	93,742
6	Columbus, OH	75,312
7	Minneapolis	68,084
8	Detroit	67,524
9	Boston	58,742
10	Los Angeles	58,163

Source: Based on "The Service 500," Fortune, May 31, 1993, pp. 199-230.

The global economy despite its word is sharply managed and directed by few leading
countries. It is at the same time an economy that involves more and more nations in the world
but the polarization between the ruled countries and the rulers is becoming sharper.
   "During the 1970s and 1980s there was an important shift from an international to a more global
economy. In the international economy, individuals and firms from different countries traded goods and
services across national boundaries, and the trade was closely regulated by sovereign states.
In the global economy goods and services are produced and marketed by an oligopolistic web of global
corporate networks whose operations span national boundaries but are only loosely regulated by
states." [10]

Market for goods and services are becoming increasingly globalized. But the actual trading
units are not countries, but firms, and networks of firms. (Castells 1996)
From these data it appears clearer and clearer that the phenomenon of globalization tends to
be regulated by few countries: The USA, the UK, Japan, France and Germany and within these
countries New York, London and Tokyo, Frankfurt and Paris are the centres. In these cities
then are located the most powerful firms in the world that are able to control the entire financial
activities.

---

[10] Paul L. Knox and Peter J. Taylor (ed), 1995, World cities in a world system,
Cambridge University press, Cambridge

Top Five Global Command Centers Based on Corporations,
Banks, Stock Markets, and Advertising Agencies Rankings, 1996
and 1997

Rank	City[a]	Corporations (1997)	Banks (1996)	Stock Markets (1996)[b]	Advertising Agencies (1997)
1	Tokyo	1	1	3	2
2	New York	2	6	2	1
3	London	6	4	1	3
4	Paris	3	2	5	5
5	Frankfurt	11	3	4	11

a. Cities ranked within the top 20 in the corporation (based on *Fortune*'s Global 500) and
bank tables, within the top 5 stock markets and within the top 17 advertising agencies.

b. Based on the number of listed companies (domestic and foreign).

Source: Short and Kim, *Globalization and the City* (1999:36).

If we also look at the top cities ranked by stock market value in 1990 and 1997, it is difficult to
predict a real phenomenon of globalization.
The increase in the value of NYSE (New York Stock Exchange) is overwhelming compared to
any other; Tokyo the second city has a stock market value of 1/3 of the one of New York.
Finally London and New York account for well over half of the global currency exchange
market. (Sassen 2000)

Is it still possible to speak in terms of globalization?
Or should we instead talk about a process of "oligarchy-zation" where three countries: the USA,
the UK and Japan own around the 75% of the global stock market value.
(*Source:* Based on Meridian Securities Markets, *World Stock Exchange Fact Book 1998*)
It is also important to consider the fact that cities as London, New York, Tokyo are not
competing with each other but instead they are collaborating, in avoiding radical changes in the
global economy, and to maintain their leadership (Sassen 2000).

Spatial and social inequalities

Globalization does operate in an extensive way but rather in a punctual way on a global scale.

The population in the developing countries is moving from villages to the big megalopolises at an impressive rate, for instance 60 new inhabitants move to Manila every hour!
(Source: F. Moriconi-Ebrard, 2000)
The shift from rural population to urban population in the developing countries
"Was substantially promoted by the expansion of the world market for commodities and the foreign direct investment of multinational organization". [11]

The economic globalization has had a range of impacts on cities in the developing countries, in some cases, it has contributed to the development of new growth poles outside the major urban agglomerations, this has often been the case with the development of export manufacturing zones, agriculture for export and tourism.
In others, it has actually raised the weight of primate urban agglomerations.
Production zones, centres for tourism, and major business and financial centres are three types of sites for the implantation of global processes. Beyond these sites there is a vast terrain containing cities, towns, and villages that is increasingly unhinged from this new international growth dynamic. (Sassen 2000)

In Europe globalisation affects cities in terms of "connectivity".
Every European city has been investing a lot of energies in the accessibility to its own area, in its infrastructures, in becoming part of a trans-national network.
What is important to understand is that the traditional national urban networks are changing.
Cities that were once dominant in their nation may lose their importance, while cities in border regions or transportation hubs may gain a new role.
Furthermore, the new European global cities may capture some of the business, demands for specialized services and investments that previously went to national capitals or major provincial cities.
Cities that are well connected are gaining population again after the decline in the 1960s and 1970s and also are acquiring a significant economic growth; this is mainly due to the shift to services, most particularly the ascendance of finance and specialized services.
As a consequence cities as Hamburg, Amsterdam and Copenhagen, are becoming new centres in the world net, while other cities in peripheral areas as Marseilles, Naples and Manchester continue to lose in terms of population and economical activities.
Two tendencies contributing to new forms of inequality among cities are visible in the geography and characteristics of urban systems. On one hand, there is growing articulation at a trans-national level among cities. Some cities have an overlapping of hierarchies that operate at more than one level: London belongs to a national urban system or hierarchy, to a trans-national European system, and to a global system. On the other hand, cities and areas outside these hierarchies tend to become peripherals (Sassen 2000).

What comes clearer is that the global financial industry tends to consolidate few centres. In the USA for instance New York concentrates all the leading investments banks with only one major international financial centre: Chicago.
The ascendance of the new finance and the possibility that this can earn super-profits has also influenced large sectors of the urban economy. High prices and profit levels in the

---

[11] Saskia Sassen, 2000, Cities in a world economy (second edition),
Pine Forge press, Thousand Oaks, London, Delhi

internationalised sector and its ancillary activities, such as top-of-the-line restaurants and hotels, have made it increasingly difficult for other sectors to compete for space and investments.

Cities as New York, London, Tokyo, Paris, Frankfurt, Amsterdam, Zurich, Sydney and Hong Kong are global cities because they host the major international financial and business centres. The intensity of transactions among these cities, particularly through financial markets, flows of services, and investment has increased sharply.

Globalization stands in most of the cases for concentration in strategic spots.
Beside this geographical inequality there is another, a social one generated by the rapid growth of the financial industry and of highly specialized services that generate not only high-level technical and administrative jobs but also low-wage unskilled jobs.

Average Real Hourly Wages of All Workers, by Education in the United States, 1973 to 1997 (1997 Dollars)

Year	Less Than High School	High School	Some College	College	Advanced Degree
1973	$11.21	$12.82	$14.16	$18.60	$22.67
1974	$10.96	$12.48	$13.62	$18.02	$23.03
1975	$10.65	$12.38	$13.68	$17.87	$23.00
1976	$10.85	$12.48	$13.88	$17.77	$22.37
1977	$10.91	$12.38	$13.47	$17.56	$22.31
1978	$10.76	$12.40	$13.66	$17.55	$22.22
1979	$11.15	$12.49	$13.61	$17.43	$21.42
1980	$10.80	$12.07	$13.34	$17.16	$20.98
1981	$10.55	$11.91	$13.22	$17.20	$20.85
1982	$10.31	$11.90	$13.18	$17.41	$21.39
1983	$10.12	$11.78	$13.07	$17.48	$21.82
1984	$10.00	$11.66	$13.20	$17.68	$22.22
1985	$ 9.91	$11.70	$13.33	$17.95	$22.66
1986	$ 9.91	$11.72	$13.32	$17.66	$21.90
1987	$ 9.71	$11.65	$13.28	$17.73	$21.94
1988	$ 9.63	$11.59	$13.09	$17.56	$21.80
1989	$ 9.38	$11.36	$13.19	$17.88	$23.24
1990	$ 9.15	$11.18	$13.19	$18.00	$23.30
1991	$ 8.99	$11.13	$13.07	$17.69	$23.55
1992	$ 8.86	$11.07	$12.52	$18.04	$23.03
1993	$ 8.72	$11.02	$12.47	$17.97	$23.22
1994	$ 8.52	$11.10	$12.36	$18.14	$24.17
1995	$ 8.25	$10.90	$12.20	$18.13	$23.90
1996	$ 8.21	$10.84	$12.18	$17.86	$23.80
1997	$ 8.22	$11.02	$12.43	$18.38	$24.07

Note: Values are adjusted for inflation using the CPI-U-X1 deflator.

Source: Economic Policy Institute analysis of U.S. Bureau of the Census, Current Population Survey data, 1998 (http://www.census.gov).

This determines a new urban configuration in the city.

In London for example to be able to purchase an average flat (one bedroom) is necessary to have 120,000 pounds, and to be able to access a mortgage is necessary to earn at least 38,000 pounds p.a. Now a staff nurse earns 18,200 while a teacher earnes19,800. (Ukinfo 2001) As a result of this social injustice more and more people are forced to relocate themselves far from the centre, in the suburb and commute daily from long distances to their work.

The existence of all these people that is essential to make the city work is threatened by finance and specialized services that can have super-profits pushing housing prices to an extremely high cost.

The rapid development of an international property market has made this disparity even worse. It means that real estate prices at the centre of New York are more connected to prices in London or Frankfurt than to the overall real estate market in the city.

We also have to consider that many Germans, Dutch and U.S. investors are buying properties in central London and in major cities around the world, forcing prices up because of the competition and raise them even further to sell at a profit.

"How can a small commercial operation in these cities compete with such investors and the prices they can command?" [12]

The conditions for ongoing inequality can also be seen in projections for educational requirements. In the USA over half of all jobs require only high school diploma or less. While highly educated people especially in the law and financial sector see their salary increase rapidly, low-skilled manual workers see their wages stagnate (Sassen 2000).

So if it is true that some cities are gaining a global role in the world economy, and their centres is getting packed with financial firms it is also true that within these cities social inequalities are growing and getting more polarized.

I would like to finish by showing some interesting data about the world's condition today.

-While the worldwide wealth has increased from 21 trillion US dollars in 1990 to 30 trillion dollars in 1999 the illiteracy among men older then 15 increased in the same period from 18% to 32%.

- 40% of the world's population does not have electricity.
- 47% of the world's population lives on less than two US dollars a day.
- 33% of children under the age of 5 suffer from malnutrition.
- The foreign debt of developing countries has grown more than 6 times its amount since 1970, totalling 2.8 trillion dollars in 1999.
- Developed countries represent 86% of private expenditure consumption.
- The total wealth of the 200 richest people is 1.14 trillion dollars, almost the 4% of the worldwide wealth. (Sources: World Bank, WorldWatch Institute, World Health Organization, UNESCO, Unicef)

The distribution of wealth appears to be a matter that invests lesser and lesser people.

---

[12] Saskia Sassen, 2000, Cities in a world economy (second edition), Pine Forge press, Thousand Oaks, London, Delhi

Bibliography

Francine Fort, Michel Jacques (ed) 2001, <u>Mutations,</u>
Actar, Barcelona ISBN 84-95273-51-9

Saskia Sassen, 2000, <u>Cities in a world economy (second edition),</u>
Pine Forge press, Thousand Oaks, London, Delhi ISBN 0-7619-8666-9

Manuel Castells, 1996, <u>The rise of the network society (second edition),</u>
Blackwell Publishers, Oxford, ISBN 0-631-22140-9

Paul L. Knox and Peter J. Taylor (ed), 1995, <u>World cities in a world system,</u>
Cambridge University press, Cambridge, ISBN 0-521-48740-7

Webster's encyclopedic unabridged dictionary of the English language, 1989, Portland House,
New York

Collins English Dictionary, 1987, Collins, London